Great Lawyer Stories

Great Lawyer Stories

From Courthouse to Jailhouse, Tall Tales, Jokes, and Anecdotes

by Bill Adler

A Citadel Press Book

PUBLISHED BY CAROL PUBLISHING GROUP

A Citadel Press Book
Published by Carol Publishing Group
Citadel Press is a registered trademark of Carol
Communications, Inc.
Editorial Offices: 600 Madison Avenue, New York, N.Y. 10022
Sales & Distribution Offices: 120 Enterprise Avenue, Secaucus,
N.J. 07094
In Canada: Canadian Manda Group, P.O. Box 920 Station U,
 Toronto, Ontario M8Z 5P9
Queries regarding rights and permissions should be addressed to
Carol Publishing Group, 600 Madison Avenue, New York, N.Y. 10022

Carol Publishing Group books are available at special discounts
for bulk purchases, for sales promotions, fund raising, or
educational purposes. Special editions can be created to specifications.
For details contact: Special Sales Department, Carol Publishing
Group, 120 Enterprise Avenue, Secaucus, N.J. 07094

Manufactured in the United States of America
10 9 8 7 6 5 4 3 2 1

Library of Congress Cataloging-in-Publication Data

Great lawyer stores : from courthouse to a jailhouse, tall tales,
 jokes, and anecdotes / [compiled] by Bill Adler.
   p. cm.
"A Citadel Press book."
ISBN 0–8065–1373–X
1. Lawyers—United States—Humor. 2. Law—United States—Humor.
3. Courts—United States—Humor. 4. Lawyers—United States—
Anecdotes. 5. Law—United States—Anecdotes. 6. Courts—United
States—Anecdotes. I. Adler, Bill, 1956–
K184.G735 1992
349.73'0207—dc20
[347.300207]   92–20863

I am most greatful to the creative assistance of Virginia Fay in the writing of this book. Without her this book would not have been possible.

Contents

Introduction

This book is dedicated to all those who love a great lawyer story.

We have tried to select the very best of courthouse humor—tall tales, jokes, and anecdotes about the legal profession.

I am confident there is material in this book that aspiring lawyers, or distinguished jurists, or senior partners can use in their next speech or at their next dinner party.

The material is designed to entertain and perhaps even to inform.

Bill Adler
New York City
1992

Great Lawyer Stories

1

Cases

Sometimes witty judges are faced with situations they simply can't ignore. In the Matter of Charlotte K., 102 Misc 2d. 848, 427 N.Y.S. 2d. 370 (1980), in which a minor used her girdle to hide shoplifted merchandise. She was charged with using her girdle as a burglary tool.

Subsequently the court wrote the following:

"Is a girdle a burglar's tool or is that stretching the plain meaning of Penal Law Sec. 140? This elastic issue of first impression arises out of a charge that the respondent shoplifted certain items...by dropping them into her girdle.

"Basically [the prosecutor] argues that respondent used her girdle as a kangaroo does her pouch, thus adapting it beyond its maiden form. The [public defender] snaps back charging that with this artificial explanation of Sec. 140's meaning, the foundation of...counsel's argument plainly sags."

* * *

A Milton, Forida, woman was allowed by a federal tax court to deduct travel expenses to and from her job, a deduction not ordinarily allowed. She proved that her "job" was as a blood donor, and that the travel was the only way to get her profit-making product to market. (However, the court disallowed her claim for a "mineral depletion allowance" for the minerals in her blood, finding that Congress intended that deduction only for mining activities.)

* * *

DOES A PREGNANT WOMAN, DRIVING ALONE, QUALIFY AS A "CAR POOL"?

California freeways frequently reserve a special lane for car pools and buses during rush hours, posting signs which warn: "A car pool requires two or more persons occupying the vehicle." The defendant was ticketed for driving alone in the car pool lane during rush hours. When she appeared in court, obviously pregnant, she contended that her unborn child was a "person," therefore she qualified as a "car pool." The prosecution protested that police officers were in no poisition to confirm the validity of a driver's claim she was pregnant, suggesting, "A woman could stuff pillows up her dress."

HELD: An unborn child is a person for purposes of forming a two-person car pool.

People v. Yaeger
Orange County Municipal Court

*   *   *

Life in the fast lane was a problem, however, for the driver of a mortuary van. The driver claimed that four frozen cadavers he was transporting qualified his vehicle for the car pool lane. Orange County Municipal Court Judge Richard Stanford, Jr., ruled that passengers must be alive to qualify.

People v. Hanshew
Orange County Municipal Court

2

Clients

A lawyer who had won a seemingly impossible case for his client wired exuberantly: JUSTICE HAS TRIUMPHED!

The client unhesitatingly replied: APPEAL THE CASE!

A seasoned pro loses on a robbery trial. Client turns to him and says, "Well, where do we go from here?"

The pro replies, "Son, you're going to prison. I'm going to lunch!"

Normalcy is when you run out of money.
Insolvency is when you run out of excuses.
Bankruptcy is when you run out of town.

Martin J. Yudkowitz

Plaintiff claims that the hospital was negligent in its care for the plaintiff, that the decedent's condition was incorrectly diagnosed, that the surgery was inadequately performed, and that improper precautions were taken to avoid internal bleeding. Other than that, she had no complaints about the hospital.

Plaintiff states that immediately prior to the accident she turned into a shopping center. This evidently was a mistake. She had intended to turn into a gas station.

To save the state the expense of trial, your honor, my client has escaped.

"Why did you throw the pot of geraniums at the plaintiff?"
    "Because of an advertisement, your honor."
    "What advertisement?"
    "'Say it with flowers.'"

LAWYER: (over the telephone): "They can't put you in jail for that."
CLIENT: "Oh, yeah? Where do you think I'm phoning from?"

"You're a cheat!" shouted the lawyer's client. "You're a blackguard! You've kept me hanging for months and got rich on my case alone!"
    "That's gratitude!" said the aggrieved lawyer sadly. "And I just named my new yacht after you!"

"Now," said the lawyer, "are you sure you told me all the truth? For if I am to defend you I must know everything."

"Yep. Sure. I told you everything."

"Good. I think I can easily get you acquitted for you have an excellent alibi that proves you are innocent, beyond a doubt, of this robbery. Now you are sure, absolutely sure, that you've told me everything?"

"Yeah. All except where I hid the money."

An Abilene, Texas, funeral home was not too pleased to find its Yellow Pages ad listed under "Frozen Foods—Wholesale." The telephone company was sued for over $300,000, the home claiming that it was held up to public ridicule because the ad was not proofread and placed more appropriately under "Funeral Directors." Also alleged were the receipt of numerous crank calls, including a man who asked, "What meat is on special for the day."

No matter how much the government fights it, organized crime just seems to get more organized every day. The police pulled in a Mob kingpin recently and reminded him he had the right to make a phone call.

"Just fax the arrest report to my lawyer," the mobster said calmly.

CLIENT: I'll give you $500 if you do the worrying for me.

LAWYER: Fine. Now where is the $500?

CLIENT: That is your first worry.

One thug was having a rough time getting an attorney. Each time a lawyer learned that he hadn't stolen the money, the lawyer quit!

An absent-minded attorney rose to defend a client, and, intent on winding up the proceedings promptly and reaching the country club, got off on the wrong foot.

"This man on trial, gentlemen of the jury," he bumbled, "bears the reputation of being the most unconscionable and depraved scoundrel in the state..."

An assistant whispered frantically, "That's your client you're talking about."

Without one second's hesitation, the lawyer continued smoothly, "...but what outstanding citizen ever lived who has not been vilified and slandered by envious contemporaries?"

3

Correspondence

This eighty-nine-year-old plaintiff claims that as a result of the accident, she can no longer dance.

Have you ever suffered a *partial* loss of smell in either ear? If so, state how long a period of time before you were able to smell fully again, and out of which ear.

If your answer to the preceding interrogatory is in the affirmative, state whether or not such loss of smell was rectified by the use of a hearing aid.

We requested that the trial in this matter be held in the early fall. The judge concurred and set a date of April 6th.

Plaintiff was formerly employed as a crook, but is presently out of work.

Please review the enclosed interrogatories and then sing them.

Please notify us immediately if you do not receive this letter.

It appears that we will have a difficult time obtaining a defense verdict if this case is tried before a live jury.

We are refraining from providing you with copies of the medical records, which are enclosed.

Enclosed is our status report on this matter. Please be advised that this case is a mess.

Please find enclosed copies of the plaintiff.

Plaintiff weighs 125 pounds with a driver's license.

The bus operator claims he ran over the plaintiff because he was behind schedule.

The court, in its discretion, is permitted to strike irrelevant, redundant, and redundant matters.

He suffered a fracture to his left foreman.

* * *

Correspondence

ACCIDENT REPORTS

The guy was all over the road. I had to swerve a number of times before I hit him.

I was on my way to the doctor's with rear-end trouble when my universal joint gave way causing me to have an accident.

I was thrown from my car as it left the road. I was later found in a ditch by some stray cows.

* * *

PROBATION REPORTS

Although somewhat large for his age, Tony appears somewhat smaller than he actually is.

The boy was arrested for petty theft after the Earl Warren Junior High was broken in two.

This boy, a surfer, gets along well with his pier group.

The defendant is charged with the theft of a roast from a meat market. The defendant acknowledged that before going to the market he pre-heated his oven.

* * *

You might expect comedians to make jokes about lawyers—but would you believe a U.S. Supreme Court Justice, even if he was partly serious?

"The problem with lawyers is they tend to make law far more serious and somber—and unintelligible—than it really is," said Supreme Court Justice Antonin Scalia. He was in Snowmass Village, Colorado, to speak to the ninety-second annual convention of the state's Bar Association.

Scalia lectured them on the art of writing legal briefs. "A brief," he said, "has two parts: a summary of arguments, and the arguments." "Judges read the summaries," he said, "so they should be written 'in English.' The rest can be in 'legal English.'"

"Normal English will not do," he said. "It is essential to legal English that one write as pompously as possible...."

4

𝕯efendants

A lawyer was defending a man accused of housebreaking, and said to the court:

"Your Honor, I submit that my client did not break into the house at all. He found the parlor window open and merely inserted his right arm and removed a few trifling articles. Now, my client's arm is not himself, and I fail to see how you can punish the whole individual for an offense committed by only one of his limbs."

The judge considered this argument for several moments, and then replied: "That argument is very well put. Following it logically, I sentence the defendant's arm to one year's imprisonment. He can accompany it or not, as he chooses."

The defendant smiled, and with his lawyers's assistance unscrewed his cork arm, and leaving it in the dock, walked out.

DEFENDANT: As God is my judge, I didn't do it. I'm not guilty.

JUDGE: He isn't, I am. You did. You are.

JUDGE: Why did you steal the pearl necklace from the jeweller's shop window?

PRISONER: Because it had on it "Avail yourself of this splendid opportunity," and I couldn't resist it!

JUDGE: Does the defendant realize he was driving down a one-way street?

DEFENDANT: I was only driving one way, your honor.

JUDGE: Didn't you see the arrows?

DEFENDANT: Arrows?! I didn't even see the Indians.

* * *

VARIATIONS ON A THEME

WESTERN LAWYER: Well, Zeb, so you want me to defend you? Have you got any money?

ZEB: No, suh, I got no money, but I got me a new palomino pony.

WESTERN LAWYER: Well, you can certainly raise money on a palomino pony. Now let's see, just what do they accuse you of stealing?

ZEB: A palomino pony.

The prisoner had sent for the town's leading lawyer.

"Have you anything by way of cash for my fee?" the attorney wanted to know.

"No, but I've got a new Ford car."

"Well, that's fine. That will do. And what is the charge they are holding against you?"

The prisoner replied, "Stealing a new Ford car."

* * *

JUDGE: I'm afraid I'll have to lock you up for the night.
DEFENDANT: What's the charge?
JUDGE: There's no charge. It's part of the service.

The judge who was about to deliver a severe sentence looked at the defendant in the dock and began: "This robbery was consummated in an adroit and skillful manner."

The prisoner blushed and interrupted: "Come now, your honor. No flattery, please."

Despite the best effort of lawyer Newman, the defendant was convicted of murder and sentenced to the electric chair. On the night before the execution he called Newman for any final words of advice.

The lawyer promptly replied, "Don't sit down."

Ignoring the defendant's impassioned arguments, a justice of the peace ruled against a shopowner in small claims court. Still boiling with rage, the fellow reached for his wallet and handed over the sum in question, and then demanded a receipt.

"Calm down, buddy," soothed the judge. "You don't

need a receipt. The court record will clearly indicate the claim has been settled."

"I still want a receipt, and I want it now," he sputtered.

"Fine, fine," said the judge, "but why does it matter so much to you?"

"Because when I die and go to Heaven, St. Peter's going to ask me if the judgment was paid. And if my word isn't good enough and he demands a receipt, I'm damned if I'm gonna hunt for you all over Hell."

JUDGE: Have you ever been up before me?
ACCUSED: I don't know. What time do you get up?

JUDGE: You've been convicted ten times of this same crime. Aren't you ashamed of youself?
DEFENDANT: No, your Honor. I don't believe one should be ashamed of one's convictions.

"Why couldn't you two men settle this case out of court?" the judge asked.

"We tried to," one of the men replied. "But the police came and broke it up."

The defendant was rattled by the prosecutor's driving questions and constant interruptions. "If you don't mind," he said to the prosecutor, "I'd like to tell my story in my lawyer's own words."

A woman charged with theft showed up in court without an attorney.

30

"Do you want me to assign you an attorney?" asked the presiding judge.

"No, sir," said the defendant.

"But you are entitled to an attorney and you might as well have the benefit of legal services," said the portly jurist.

"If it's all the same with you," said the defendant, "I'd like to throw myself upon the ignorance of the court."

Did you hear about the thief who was caught in the rubber factory?

The judge sent him up for a stretch.

JUDGE: What do you mean by bringing a ladder into this room?

CRIMINAL: I want to take my case to a higher court.

A burglar alarm sent out its piercing wail in the dark of a December night, and the police arrived just in time to collar the burglar as he was leaving the premises with a satchel full of loot. Soon he was in court, facing a grim-looking judge.

"Did you have an accomplice?" asked the magistrate.

"What's an accomplice?"

"A partner. In other words, did you commit this crime by yourself?"

"What else?" demanded the culprit. "Who can get reliable help these days?"

"What, you here again?" demanded the judge.

"It wasn't my fault," said Goldberg. "The man bought a garment and then complained I didn't give enough change. It's a lie!"

31

The judge shook his head. "Mr. Goldberg, last year you were in this court because a customer accused you of wrapping up a cheaper suit than he had actually ordered. Then you were brought in again for doing business without a license. After that," continued the judge, reading from a thick dossier, "you had a fistfight with your competitor across the street. This year, so far, you've been in here twice—and each time you have been found guilty. I wonder, Mr. Goldberg, if you realize how much trouble you are to this court?"

"Well, look who's talking!" snapped Goldberg indignantly. "I'm troubling *you?*"

A pair of Michigan robbers entered a record shop brandishing revolvers and ordering, "Nobody move." When his partner moved, the second bandit shot him in the head at point-blank range.

Two bank thieves, armed with shotguns, burst into a Los Angeles bank and ordered everyone to lie down on the floor. All employees and customers complied, leaving no one to fetch the money. The robbers hesitated and then fled, penniless.

A man was arraigned for assault and battery and brought before the judge.

JUDGE: What is your name, occupation, and what are you charged with?
PRISONER: My name is Sparks; I am an electrician, and I'm charged with battery.
JUDGE: (After recovering his equilibrium) Officer, put this guy in a dry cell.

Defendants

JUDGE: Order! Order in the court!
DEFENDANT: I'll have a ham sandwich!

Portsmouth, Rhode Island, police charged Gregory
Rosa, twenty-five, with a string of vending machine robberies after he inexplicably fled from police when they
spotted him loitering around a vending machine. Police
were pretty sure they had their man when Rosa later
tried to post bail using $400 in coins.

JUDGE: The next man who raises his voice in the
             court will be thrown out.
PRISONER: Hip, hip hooray!

While working his criminal calendar, the judged called
the case of *People v. Steven Lewon Crook.* The bailiff
opened the door to the holding cell and called "Crook,
come forward." Five prisoners walked from the cell into
the courtroom.

The defendant, charged with arson, missed a court
appearance.
THE COURT: Where were you?
DEFENDANT: In the hospital.
THE COURT: Why?
DEFENDANT: Smoke inhalation.

5

Divorces

After being married to Nathan for thirty years, his wife, Rebecca, was suing him for a divorce. On the witness stand, she said, "My husband curses me in his sleep!"

Nathan yelled to the judge, "Your honor, that's a lie! I'm not asleep!"

Her lawyer phoned Mrs. Gitkin and said excitedly, "I told you when I took your divorce case that I would rather avoid lengthy litigation and try to make an out-of-court settlement. Well, I've just concluded a meeting with your husband's attorney and we have worked out a settlement that, I believe, is eminently fair to both of you!"

"Fair to both!" exploded Mrs. Gitkin. "For that, I had to hire a lawyer! That I could have done myself!"

Ninety-four-year-old Mrs. Hatcher showed up at her lawyer's office one Monday morning. "I want you to begin divorce proceedings," she announced.

The lawyer was aghast. When he regained his composure, he said, "Mrs. Hatcher, you and your husband have been married for over seventy years. What in the world could have happened to make you want to get divorced at this stage in your life?"

Mrs. Hatcher looked him squarely in the eye. She cleared her throat and said, "We wanted to wait until all the children were dead."

An actress asked her attorney how much he'd charge for handling her divorce. The attorney said, "Fifty thousand, or three for a hundred."

Orange County, California, Superior Court clerks discovered in 1989 that they had failed to complete paperwork to make nearly five hundred pre-1985 divorce judgments final, thus leaving the parties still legally married. The worst-case scenario for one husband occurred after an error by an Arizona court in 1990 when a woman was ruled one-fourth owner of her ex-husband's $2.2 million lottery jackpot because a paperwork error delayed the official divorce date eleven days, during which time he won the lottery.

"Hello, Abe, how's the law business?"

"Don't even ask! It's been so long since I had a client, I divorced my wife last month just so I would have a case."

Divorces

A husband was suing his wife for divorce and his lawyer was determined to put her in as bad a light as possible.

"What line of work were you in before you married my client?" he asked when she was on the witness stand.

"I was a stripper in a burlesque," she answered promptly.

"Aha! And do you consider that a decent occupation for a respectable lady?"

"Well, to tell the truth, I was proud of my work in comparison to what my father did for a living."

The attorney smiled, sure now that he had already won his case. "Tell the court, please, just what it was that your father did for a living. Speak up, Madam!"

"He was a lawyer!" she snapped.

Hear about the woman who sent out 1500 perfumed erotic Valentines signed "Guess who?"

She's a divorce lawyer.

Arlene got on the phone to her lawyer and declared, "I want a divorce."

"Well, this is kind of sudden," the lawyer commented. "Do you have grounds?"

"Sure do—the apartment in the city and a beach house on Fire Island."

The lawyer persisted. "What I mean is, do you have some kind of grudge?"

"Not exactly. But there's parking underneath the building," Arlene replied brightly.

"That's not what I mean," he said, growing exasperated. "Your husband Joe, does he beat you up or something?"

"Oh, no, I'm the first one up every morning."

"Arlene!" yelled the lawyer, "can you just tell me why you want a divorce?"

"Certainly: It's because I just can't carry on a decent conversation with the man.

Forced by a team of cunning and venal attorneys into a disasterous divorce settlement, Swenson decided to try and forget his woes by taking a vacation out West. Putting distance between himself and his problems didn't help much, though, so Swenson went into the nearest town and started to drown his sorrows in the corner tavern. He fell to mulling over his divorce again, and soon blurted out, "Goddamn lawyers—they're all a bunch of horses' asses."

"For God's sake, mister," said the bartender, rushing over and addressing Swenson in a stage whisper, "don't say things like that around here. Don't you know you're in horse country."

Love, the quest; marriage, the conquest; divorce, the inquest.

Helen Rowland, American humorist
Reflections of a Bachelor Girl, 1903

Plaque in a Manhattan lawyer's office:
FOR THE WOMAN
WHO HAS EVERYTHING
—A DIVORCE.

Divorces

Judges, as a class, display, in the matter of arranging alimony, that reckless generosity which is found only in men who are giving away someone else's cash.

P.G. Wodehouse

My wife had a fine lawyer for our divorce settlement. Perhaps you've heard of him? Highway Robber.

6

Doctors and Lawyers

A physician presented her bill to the courts as a legal way of collecting fees due from a deceased person's estate.

"Do you wish my bill sworn to?" the doctor asked.

"No," said the legalite. "Death of the deceased is sufficient evidence that you attended him professionally."

Visiting New York City for a medical convention, a doctor from the University of Utah took the afternoon off to do some shopping. Wandering into a little antiques store, he came across a curious brass sculpture of a rat and inquired as to the price. "I've sold that piece twice and it's been returned twice—so I'll let you have it for four hundred dollars. It's very old."

The doctor paid and headed out with his purchase in a bag under his arm. Not much later he noticed the shadowy forms of hundreds of live rats scuttling along in the gutters. A little while later the rats had swelled in number to several thousand, and it became evident they were following the doctor. His astonishment turned to disgust and alarm as the rat pack grew to fill up the whole street, so he picked up speed and headed east. When he reached the river, he chucked the brass rat right in, and to his considerable relief the horde of rats followed it to a watery death.

The next morning the doctor was the very first customer in the antiques store.

"No way, buddy, I'm not taking it back a third time," the owner staunchly maintained.

"Relax, I'm not bringing the rat back," soothed the doctor. "I just wanted to know...do you have a brass lawyer?"

Bumper sticker:
SUPPORT YOUR LOCAL LAWYER—
SEND YOUR KID TO MEDICAL SCHOOL

An attorney arguing a malpractice suit against two doctors in Bloomsburg, Pennsylvania, had just finished telling the jury of the defendants' "lack of skill, care, diligence and good judgment, "when he suddenly collapsed from an apparent heart attack. The defendants, Dr. Ala al-Mashat and Dr. Ferdinand Szabo, revived seventy-one-year-old John Crisman with an assist from Dr. Phillip Breen, a surgeon who testified against them. When Crisman recovered after seven minutes of mouth-to-mouth resuscitation and heart stimulation, Dr. al-

Mashat told him, "It's a good thing you sued good doctors."

Standing around the grave of a departed friend are an anthropologist, a doctor, and a lawyer.

When the eulogies are over, the anthropologist suggests that they all put some money in the coffin, as was the practice of some ancient tribes he has been studying.

The anthropologist pulls out a $100 bill and deposits it lovingly in the coffin. Not to be outdone, the doctor also pulls out a $100 bill and deposits it in the coffin.

The lawyer writes a check for $300, puts it in the coffin and removes the $200 cash.

"Everyone in my family follows the medical profession," noted Smith. "They're lawyers."

Commonly, physicians, like beer, are best when they are old; and lawyers, like bread, when they are young and new.

> Thomas Fuller
> *The Holy State:*
> *The Good Advocate* (1642)

A man arrived in the emergency room and proceeded immediately to the Intensive Care Unit. The deponent assumed the man was a doctor because he was wearing a golf outfit.

A doctor and a lawyer are talking at a party. A woman interrupts them, complaining to the doctor that her arm hurts. She explains the symptoms, rolls up her sleeve to show him, and he looks at it and tells her what to do. After she leaves, he says in exasperation to the lawyer, "I never know what to do in a situation like that. Should I send her a bill or not."

The lawyer tells him to send her a bill. So the next day, the doctor sends the woman a bill, and the lawyer sends the doctor a bill.

DOCTOR: Now I don't mean to say that all lawyers are crooks, but you've got to admit that your profession doesn't make angels of men.

LAWYER: Quite true. You doctors certainly have the best of us there.

Have you heard the one about the triple wedding ceremony in which three women executives married, respectively, a doctor, a lawyer, and an adman. The couples jet to the Bahamas for a honeymoon on Paradise Island. And the next moning the three brides gather on the balcony of the spacious condo they're sharing to compare notes on connubial bliss. (The husbands, naturally, have left early to play golf.)

"It was terrific last night," smiles Mrs. Doctor. "Though to be honest, at the beginning he was pretty anatomical about everything. He had to say what went where and why."

"Our evening was incredible," beamed Mrs. Lawyer. "But before we got started we had to take out a legal pad and jot down a list of pros and cons."

The expectantly look over to Mrs. Adman, who burst into tears. "I don't have anything to say," she sobbed.

"All he did was sit on the end of the bed and tell me how good it was going to be."

A big corporation is interviewing prospects for a new member of the Board of Directors. There are three candidates: an engineer, a doctor, and a lawyer. There is one question the candidate must answer.

The selection committee first calls the engineer. "What is 2 + 2?" they ask.

The engineer pulls out his slide rule, fiddles around with it for a while, and announces, "The answer to 2 + 2 lies somewhere between 3 and 5."

They call the doctor in and ask him, "What is 2 + 2?"

The doctor rubs his chin and thinks for a minute, and then says, "My preliminary diagnosis is that the answer is four, but I'll have to run some tests and get back to you."

The lawyer comes in next. They ask him, "What is 2 + 2?"

The lawyer looks around the room and asks quietly, "Can anyone hear what we're saying in here?" The committee members shake their heads. The lawyer moves closer and says: "What do you want it to be?"

An old man is dying, gathers his doctor, minister, and attorney and says, "Boys, I am going to take it with me! I am giving each of you an envelope with $20,000 in it. Throw it in my casket before they close it."

After the funeral, the three walk back to their cars. The minister breaks down in tears. "The parsonage needed a new roof and there was only $10,000 in my envelope when I threw it in!"

The doctor then confessed about his need for a new X-ray machine and that there was only $5,000 in his envelope.

The attorney fixed both with a steely, gimlet gaze and said: "Thieves, hypocrites, I want you to know that there was a check for the full $20,000 in my envelope when I threw it in."

Every trial lawyer's nightmare—the unexpected answer by a witness.

PLAINTIFF'S LAWYER:	What doctor treated you for the injuries you sustained while at work?
PLAINTIFF:	Dr. J.
PLAINTIFF'S LAWYER:	And what kind of physician is Dr. J.?
PLAINTIFF:	Well, I'm not sure, but I remember you said he was a good plaintiff's doctor.

Asked to identify himself, a witness in a case began pompously, "I employ myself as a surgeon."

"But does anyone else employ you as a surgeon?"

There are abuses incident to every branch of industry, to every profession. It would not be thought very just or wise to arraign the honorable professions of law and physic, because the one produces the pettifogger, and the other the quack.

Henry Clay

7

Epitaphs

Perhaps you've heard about the genealogy class visiting a local cemetary that happened upon a headstone reading: Here lies a lawyer and an honest man.

"Why, look, class," observed the professor. "There are two people buried in this plot."

Here's one on John Strange, the lawyer:

> Here lies an
> Honest Lawyer
>
> That is Strange

Occasionally, professional people have taken as their epitaphs phrases from their earthly work.

One doctor, for example, finally flouted the rule that prohibits physicians from advertising. She had the following carved on her headstone: "Office Upstairs."

Not to be outdone, a lawyer's gravestone read: "Final Decree."

Epitah, Massachusetts churchyard:

> Beneath this smooth stone by
>   the bone of his bone
> Sleeps Master John Gill;
> By lies when alive this attorney
>   did thrive
> And now that he's dead he lies
>   still.

Epitaph for one Peter Robinson

Here lies the preacher, judge, and poet, Peter
Who broke the laws of God, and man, and metre.

8

Ethics

Mark Twain had just finished addressing a New England society banquet when the attorney William M. Evarts stood up with his hands in his pockets, as was his custom, and remarked: "Does it not seem unusual to this gathering that a professional humorist should really appear funny?"

Twain arose and responded in his habitual drawl: "Does it not also appear strange to this assembly that a lawyer should have his hands in his own pockets?"

A lawyer is a learned gentleman who rescues your estate from your enemies and keeps it himself.

Lord Brougham

When it was learned that old Macauley, a member of the bar for almost thirty years, had only a few days to live, his buddy Flaherty hurried over to the hospital. To his surprise, he found the patient sitting bolt upright in bed, leafing through the Bible in a frenzy.

"Take it easy, pal, calm down," Flaherty soothed. "What the hell're you up to, anyway?"

"Looking for the loopholes," gasped Macauley.

LAWYER: "When I was a boy, my highest ambition was to be a pirate."
CLIENT: "Congratulations."

"God works wonders now and then;
Behold! a lawyer, an honest man."

Benjamin Franklin

A stranger, arriving in a small New England town, approached the first native he saw and asked:

"Have you a criminal lawyer in this town?"

"Well," replied the native cautiously, "we think we have but so far we can't prove it on him."

A barrister's profession is such an uncertain thing, especially if he won't take unsavory cases.

Ibsen, *A Doll's House*

A lawyer confided to his partner that years ago he had cheated one of his clients out of $10,000. That client had just died.

"I made amends," said the lawyer. "I went to his funeral and wrote a check for $10,000 and put it in his coffin."

Ethics

Cartoon panel called "The Compassionate Attorney"—shows a client sobbing while her lawyer says, "Go ahead and cry, Mrs. Dunne. Here, have a tissue...only 75 cents."

Seems this lawyer died and went to heaven.

Certain there was some mistake, he sought out St. Peter. "I'm only thirty-five," the lawyer argued. "There's no way my time has come."

"We hardly ever make mistakes," St. Peter responded. "But I'll check the computer."

In a little while, St. Peter returned. "I checked the computer. You're 106 years old."

At this point, lawyers will laugh uproariously. The rest of us wait for something else.

That's the punch line. "Billable hours." Get it?

A boat is capsized and all the passengers are eaten by piranhas. Th only one who wasn't eaten is the lawyer. When he is picked up by another boat, the crew ask him why he thought the piranhas left him alone, to which he replies: "Professional courtesy."

Following hard on last year's proliferation of lawyer jokes, this year is not shaping up as a good year for lawyers. A poll by *New York Woman* magazine rated lawyers with used car salesmen and investment bankers as the most hated professionals.

A lawyer was consulted by a young woman in his office. The consultation took about an hour. At the end of the consultation, the client asked how much she owed. The lawyer said that he'd just send her a bill, but the woman insisted on paying right then. The lawyer quoted her a fee of $100. The woman opened her purse and gave the lawyer a $100 bill. The lawyer put the money on his desk and escorted the woman out of his office.

When the lawyer returned to his desk, he picked up the $100 bill, only to discover that it was two $100 bills stuck together. Not just one bill.

Now the lawyer had an ethical dilemna.

Should he keep the second bill or split it with his partner.

After I was graduated from Harvard, I went out to Wyoming to practice law. The Attorney General of Wyoming at that time was an old cowpuncher. He was a salty old character and loved to give advice. I went around to see him. He asked me: "Did you ever have a course in legal ethics?"

I said: "No, they don't consider it necessary to teach that at Harvard."

He said: "I am very happy to hear that, because I can in one sentence tell you all the legal ethics that any lawyer needs to know."

I said: "Go ahead, General."

He replied: "Remember this. Whenever you are involved in any litigation and it becomes apparent that someone has got to go to jail, be sure it is your client."

Thurman W. Arnold,
former Asst. Attorney General of the U.S.

9

𝕱𝖆𝖒𝖔𝖚𝖘 𝕷𝖆𝖜𝖞𝖊𝖗𝖘

My wonder is really boundless,
That among the queer cases we try,
A land-case should often be groundless,
And a water-case always be dry.

> John G. Saxe, American lawyer and poet,
> 1816–1887

"You can't earn a living defending innocent people."

> Maurice Nadjari, *New York Post*, May 8, 1975

There is never a deed so foul that something couldn't be said for the guy; that's why there are lawyers.

> Melvin Bell

I'll tell you what my daddy told me after my first trial. I asked him, "How did I do?" He paused and said, "You've got to guard against speaking more clearly than you think."

> Howard Baker, Jr.
> Interview, *Washington Post*,
> June 24, 1973

Says Sandra Day O'Connor:

"A commencement speech is a particularly difficult assignment. You're given no topic and are expected to inspire all the graduates with a stirring speech about nothing at all. I suppose that is why so many lawyers are asked to be commencement speakers."

While he was governor of Illinois, Adlai Stevenson received a letter from a congressman who complained that stationery bearing the watermark of the Illinois state seal was being used by a gambler in letters offering tips on horse racing. This was Stevenson's reply to the congressman:

"Your taste for unverified accusations reminds me of the lawyer who said to the jury: 'These are the conclusions on which I base my facts.'"

In 1961 when President Kennedy kept selecting young lawyers such as Newton Minow from Stevenson's Chicago law firm to serve in his administration, Mr. Stevenson quipped: "I regret that I have but one law firm to give to my country."

Robert F. Kennedy solemnly addressed the graduating class at Marquette University: "Years ago, I was a hard-working lawyer making $4,200 a year. I took my work home every night and was vey diligent. Ten years later I became the Attorney General of the United States. So, you see, if you want to become successful, just get your brother elected President."

Vice President Hubert Humphrey delivered this monologue before an annual Gridiron Club dinner: "And speaking of humor, it's nice to see Mr. Richard Nixon here this evening. That is, it's nice to see Mr. Nixon here this evening…as a successful lawyer!"

* * *

CLARENCE DARROW

A female client whose legal problems Darrow had solved burbled, "How can I ever show my appreciation, Mr. Darrow?"

"Ever since the Phoenicians invented money," replied Darrow, "there has been only one answer to that question."

Darrow was being interviewed for a magazine article on the reasons given by prominent men for their success. "Most of the men I've spoken to so far attribute their success to hard work," said the interviewer.

"I guess that applies to me, too," said Darrow. "I was

brought up on a farm. One very hot day I was distributing and packing down the hay which a stacker was constantly dumping on top of me. By noon I was completely exhausted. That afternoon I left the farm, never to return, and I haven't done a day of hard work since."

I have suffered from being misunderstood, but I would have suffered a hell of a lot more if I had been understood.

* * *

John Toler Norbury, 1st Earl, Irish lawyer, Chief Justice:
A Dublin attorney having died in poverty, his legal colleagues set up a subscription to pay for his funeral. Lord Norbury was asked to contribute. On inquiring what sum would be appropriate, he was told that no one else had subscribed more than a shilling. "A shilling!" exclaimed the judge, reaching into his pocket. "A shilling to bury an attorney? Why, here's a guinea! Bury one and twenty of the scoundrels."

Francis Bacon, one of the perennial favorites as the man who *really* wrote the plays attributed to William Shakespeare, was not only an accomplished essayist, but a philosopher, scientist, and lawyer as well. He reached the peak of the legal profession when he was appointed Lord Chancellor in 1618.
In one case over which Bacon presided, the defendant was a man named Hogg. The man half-jokingly argued that he should be acquitted of the charges against him because of his relationship to the judge.

"Hogg," he said, "must be kin to Bacon."

"Not until it has been hung," the Lord Chancellor replied.

From Justice Rehnquist:

"It seems a judge and a bishop were arguing over their relative importance," Rehnquist told the crowd. "The judge said, 'I'm more powerful because I can say, "You be hanged!"' The bishop said, 'I'm more powerful because I can say, "You be damned!"' 'But,' the judge said, 'when I say "You be hanged!" you are hanged.'"

From an article on Robert and Elizabeth Dole:

The Doles have been the quintessential Washington power couple. They joke that they are the only lawyers in Washington who talk to each other.

There is an accuracy that defeats itself by the over-emphasis of details.... The sentence may be so overloaded with all its possible qualifications that it will tumble down of its own weight.

> Benjamin N. Cardozo
> *Law and Literature* 7 (1931)

It is a fair summary of history to say that the safeguards of liberty have frequently been forged in controversies involving not very nice people.

> Justice Frankfurter,
> dissenting
> *United States v. Rabinowitz*
> (1950)

I abhor averages. I like the individual case. A man may have six meals one day and none the next, making an average of three meals per day, but that is not a good way to live.

Louis D. Brandeis

I used to say that, as Solicitor General, I made three arguments of every case. First came the one that I planned—as I thought, logical, coherent, complete. Second was the one actually presented—interrupted, incoherent, disjointed, disappointing. The third was the utterly devastating argument that I thought of after going to bed that night.

Robert H. Jackson
Advocacy Before the Supreme Court (1951)

Speaking at a Harvard Law School Association luncheon, Supreme Court Justice William J. Brennan, Jr., Class of '31, took the opportunity to rebut one of the arguments against broadcasting arguments at the high court. Chief Justice Warren E. Burger had objected that if the court permits radio and television coverage, networks would run snippets of the arguments instead of airing them in their entirety.

"Thank goodness," Brennan responded. "I think some of the lawyers who argue those cases will be just as happy we don't."

Another dim view of the practitioners of the law came in the mid-'80s from Derek Bok, who had run Harvard

Law School before becoming head of the whole shebang in Cambridge:

"The legal system looks grossly inequitable and inefficient, there is far too much law for those who can afford it and far too little left for those who cannot," was Bok's view.

10

Famous Nonlawyers

Some people think about sex all the time, some people think of sex some of the time and some people never think about sex: they become lawyers.

Woody Allen

For certain people, after fifty, litigation takes the place of sex.

Gore Vidal

A law firm is successful when it has more clients than partners.

Henny Youngman

If law school is so hard to get through, how come there are so many lawyers?

Calvin Trillin

Organized crime is a blight on our nation. While many young Americans are lured into a career of crime by its promise of an easy life, most criminals must work long hours, frequently in buildings without air conditioning.

Woody Allen

There was a young lawyer who showed up at a revival meeting and was asked to deliver a prayer. Unprepared, he gave a prayer straight from his lawyer's heart: "Stir up much strife amongst thy people, Lord," he prayed, "lest thy servant perish."

Senator Sam Ervin

* * *

FROM MARK TWAIN

The departmental interpreters of the laws in Washington...can always be depended on to take any reasonably good law and interpret the common sense all out of it.

Letter to H.C. Christiancy,
December 18, 1887

To succeed in the other trades, capacity must be shown; in the law, concealment of it will do.

Following the Equator, 1897,
vol. 2, ch. 1

We have an insanity plea that would have saved Cain.

Fourth of July speech, 1873

* * *

I remember it was the fashion in the army when a court-martial was being held, and the prisoner was brought in, that he should be asked if he objected to being tried by the President or to any of those officers who composed the court-martial.

On one occasion, a prisoner was so unsubordinate as to answer, "I object to the whole lot of you."

> Winston Churchill
> House of Commons, February, 1927

Necessity has no law; I know some attorneys of the same."

> Benjamin Franklin
> *Poor Richard*, 1734

Crime is only the retail department of what, in wholesale, we call penal law.

> George Bernard Shaw
> *Man and Superman*, 1903

I feel about the future of the United States whenever the president starts out on his travels the way the marshal of the Supreme Court feels about the law when he opens a session of the court. You will recall that he ends up his liturgy by saying, "God save the United States for the Court is now sitting."

> Dean Acheson, 1893–1971
> *Among Friends: Letters of*
> *Dean Acheson*, 1980

I don't want a lawyer to tell me what I cannot do; I hire him to tell me how to do what I want to do.

> J. P. Morgan, 1837–1913

They call it the Halls of Justice because the only place you get justice is in the halls.

Lenny Bruce, 1926–1966

The growing Rockefeller empire attracted the attention of the courts owing to concern over the dangers of monopolies. When William Rockefeller was required to appear in court, he decided that his best defense would lie in the refrain, "I decline to answer on the advice of counsel," as the following exchange shows:

"On the ground that the answer will incriminate you?"

"I decline to answer on the advice of counsel."

"Or is it that the answer will subject you to some forfeiture?"

"I decline to answer on the advice of counsel."

"Do you decline on the ground that the answer will disgrace you?"

"I decline to answer on the advice of counsel."

"Did your counsel tell you to stick to that one answer?"

"I decline to answer on the advice of counsel."

At that point, the whole court burst into laughter, Rockefeller included.

A countryman between two lawyers is like a fish between two cats.

Benjamin Franklin

An overpersistant insurance solicitor followed W.C. Fields into a barbershop. Fields finally exploded, "I've told you 'no' ten times now. Just to shut you up, I'll put the proposition up to my lawyer the next time I see him."

"Will you take the proper step," persisted the solicitor, "if he says it's okay?"

"I certainly will," asserted Fields. "I'll get another lawyer."

Accuracy and diligence are much more necessary to a lawyer than great comprehension of mind, or brilliancy of talent. His business is to refine, define, split hairs, look into authorities, and compare cases. A man can never gallop over the fields of law on Pegasus, nor fly across them on the wings of oratory. If he would stand on terra firma, he must descend. If he would be a great lawyer, he must first consent to become a great drudge.

Daniel Webster

Cole Porter was well known for his high living. He enjoyed traveling abroad in elegant style and he frequently ran short of funds. On one particularly extravagant venture Porter cabled the family lawyer from Europe:

Please send me $1,000.

Regards,

Cole

The lawyer sent Cole a check by return mail with the following curt note:

Cables cost money. In the future I will assume that I have your regards."

To this Porter immediately cabled back:

Regards, regards, regards,

Cole

The legal mind chiefly consists in illustrating the obvious, explaining the self-evident and expatiating on the commonplace.

> Benjamin Disraeli

Come, you of the law, who can talk if you please,
Till the man in the moon will allow it's a cheese.

> O.W. Holmes, Sr.
> Lines recited at
> Berkshire Jubilee

Whene'er he heard a tale of woe
  From client A or client B
His grief would overcome him so,
He'd scarce have strength to take his fee.

> William S. Gilbert,
> The Bab Ballads:
> Baines Carew, Gentleman

I can give it as the condensed history of most, if not all good lawyers, that they lived well and died poor.

> Daniel Webster

Sydney Smith was a diehard Tory. When he saw the Whig politician Lord Brougham arrive in the hall during a performance of Handel's *Messiah*, Smith remarked: "Here comes counsel for the other side."

Two classes of people have poor public relations—mothers-in-law and attorneys-at-law.

> Erle Stanley Gardner (A.A. Fair)
> *Some Women Won't Wait*: Foreword

Judicial reform is no sport for the short-winded.

Arthur T. Vanderbilt

America has one hundred and ten million population, 90 percent of which are lawyers, yet we can't find two of them who have not worked at some time or another for an oil company. There has been at least one lawyer engaged for every barrel of oil that ever come out of the ground.

You might wonder if they pay so much to lawyers how do they ever make anything out of the oil. They only make money out of the stock they sell. You buy a share of oil stock and for every dollar you pay, 60 percent goes for lawyers' fees, 30 percent to cover capitalization and 10 percent goes to the boring of a dry hole.

Will Rogers

Davy Crockett wrote in his autobiography that when he was a magistrate his decisions were fair because he did not know "the law," but he knew about "common justice and honesty."

In contemplating the issue of which direction—left or right—this generation will take, Illinois Senator Dirksen recalls "the days when circuit judges rode about on horseback. I am advised that down in Kentucky in those days when Abraham Lincoln was a member of the Illinois legislature, they had a judge who had a great fondness for corn liquor.

"One day," Dirksen continues, "when the judge was 'slightly mellow' he went out to throw a saddle on his horse. A young lawyer watching the operation noticed that the judge had the pommel where the cantle should be. He said, 'Your Honor, you have your saddle on backward!'

"Then, with the kind of dignity that only the judiciary can assume, the judge said, 'How in the devil do you know in what direction I am going?'"

Lawyers have been known to wrest from reluctant juries triumphant verdicts of acquittal for their clients, even when those clients, as often happens, were clearly and unmistakably innocent.

Oscar Wilde
The Decay of Lying

The minute you read something and you can't understand it, you can almost be sure that it was drawn up by a lawyer. Then if you give it to another lawyer to read and he don't know just what it means, why then you can be sure it was drawn up by a lawyer. If it's in a few words and is plain and understandable only one way, it was written by a non-lawyer.

Every time a lawyer writes something, he is not writing for posterity, he is writing so that endless others of his craft can make a living out of trying to figure out what he said, 'course perhaps he hadn't really said anything, that's what makes it hard to explain.

Will Rogers

I tell you this tale, which is strictly true.
Just by way of convincing you,

Famous Nonlawyers

How very little since things were made
They have altered in the lawyer's trade.

Rudyard Kipling
"A Truthful Song"

Lawyers are so well fortified against every emergency.
They are just like a baseball team. Now if it should happen to be a Dark Rainy Day when they argue the case,
why they have Dark Day Lawyers—men who are better
in the dark than other lawyers. They have Expert Tech-
nicality Lawyers. That is, a lawyer that don't know or
have to know anything at all about the case but who, if it
goes against his side, why he can point out that Witness
So and So had on the wrong color tie when he testified
and that in signing his name he had failed to dot one of
his "I's" and that therefore that rendered the whole of
his testimony Null and Void.

Then they have one carload of just Postponement
Lawyers. Men who can have the Falls of Niagara put
back on account of the water not being ready to come
over. Men who on the last Judgment Day will be arguing
that it should be postponed on account of Lack of
Evidence.

Then there is just the plain every day Long Winded
Lawyer who argues so long and loud that they decide in
his favor just to get him to stop. So you see, when you
have every Species of Lawyer there is, you are a hard
man to beat.

Will Rogers

11

Judges

A rather melancholy story comes by way of Boston. A successful and formidable old jurist lingered over the breakfast table reading his *Law Review*, with his wife sitting silently across the table from him—just as she had done every weekday morning for the past thirty-seven years. Seized by a sudden daredevil impulse, she spoke up. "Henry," she said, "is there anything interesting in the *Law Review* this morning?" The jurist frowned and answered gruffly, "Don't be silly!"

The judge frowned when he looked at the defendant and demanded, "Haven't I seen that face of yours before?"

"Indeed you have, your honor," said the defendant hopefully. "I gave your son violin lessons last winter."

"Ah, yes," recalled the judge. "Twenty years!"

Arthur J. Goldberg, U.S. Ambassador to the UN, relates the story of an Iowa judge who was once called to San Francisco as a substitute for an ailing colleague. One of the first cases he was called upon to decide involved admiralty law. Being from Iowa, he had no specialized knowledge in admiralty law, so he asked the litigants if they wouldn't prefer that the case be postponed until the regular judge returned. The litigants said no, they would rather have him decide it. Upon which the Iowa judge rejoined, "All right. But I want to make one thing clear. Let there be no moaning at the bar when I put out to sea."

Roy Bean, the tough "hangin'" judge of the Old West was fond of telling the story of a "smart alecky" young attorney who found himself pleading a case in the small Texas town of Sweetwater. After the lawyer's long and learned peroration, Judge Bean swept the counsel's argument aside with a peremptory wave of his gnarled hand. "What you say may well be in all them there law books, all right," snapped Bean, "But it sure as heck ain't the law in Sweetwater."

PRISONER: "It is difficult to see how I can be a forger. Why, I can't sign my own name."
JUDGE: "You are not charged with signing your own name."

A woman appeared before a judge in a traffic violation case, and it turned out she was a schoolteacher.
The judge smiled brkoadly. "Madam," he said, "I have been sitting here for years waiting for a schoolteacher to

72

stand before me. Now, you sit down at that table and write, 'I must not pass through a red light' five hundred times."

Then there was the judge who had a mirror in his chambers. Every time he passed it, he asked, "Who's the fairest of them all?:

A judge is an official who administers justice in a few words but many sentences.

A judge is a law student who marks his own examination papers.

H. L. Mencken

A Des Moines judge found himself locked outside his chambers, along with a defense lawyer and his client—due to be sentenced for burglary. Maintenance workers tried keys and drills but could not open the door. The lawyer volunteered his client—who had it open in three seconds. After thanking him for his services, the judge sentenced him to the maximum ten years in state prison.

A judge in Louisville decided a jury went "a little bit far" in recommending a sentence of 5,005 years for a man it convicted of five robberies and kidnapping. Judge Edmond Karem reduced the sentence to 1,001 years.

Re: John Philpot Curran, Irish lawyer and judge (1750-1817)
One of the high court judges had a dog he occasionally brought into the courtroom. During a trial in which

Curran was expounding a particularly involved argument, the judge, perhaps intending to indicate disregard of Curran's case, bent down and began ostentatiously to pet the dog. Curran stopped. The judge looked up inquiringly. "I beg pardon, my lord," said Curran. "I thought your lordships were in consultation."

A thief with a long record was brought before the judge.

JUDGE: Have you ever stolen?
THIEF: Now and then.
JUDGE: Where have you stolen?
THIEF: Oh, here and there.
JUDGE: Lock him up, officer.
THIEF: Hey! When do I get out of jail?
JUDGE: Oh, sooner or later.

COUNSEL: I respectfully disagree with the court.
THE COURT: Well, you have your right to disagree, but we have disagreed before and I certainly disagree with you now. The record is probably as long as you are tall with statements that have been made by you.
COUNSEL: The record should reflect that I am short, Your Honor.
THE COURT: Well, the record may also reflect that my patience with you has about reached the point of your height.

Judges

To show the proper fear that a young U.S. attorney should have for a U.S. District Court Judge:

Psychiatrist, or psychologist, died. Went to heaven. Was met at the Pearly Gates by St. Peter, who said, "I have a problem with God, and you can help me."

DOC: "A problem with God?"

ST. PETER: "Yes, I have a problem with God and if you help us out you can go back and live a hundred years on earth. It'll be wonderful. Anything you want."

DOC: "Okay. But I just can't imagine. What's wrong with God?"

ST. PETER: "He thinks he's a U.S. District Court Judge."

12

Juries

We have a criminal jury system which is superior to any in the world; and its efficiency is only marred by the difficulty of finding twelve men every day who don't know anything and can't read.

Mark Twain
Fourth of July speech, 1873

An Arizona jury awarded a Tucson woman $356,250 in damages for injuries she suffered when she fell out of the jury box while serving as a juror.

A criminal defense lawyer is making his closing argument to the jury. His client is accused of murder, but the body of the victim has never been found. He dramatically withdraws his pocket watch and announces to the jury, "Ladies and gentlemen, I have some astounding news. We have found the supposed victim of this murder alive and well, and, in exactly one minute, he will walk through that door into this courtroom."

A hushed silence falls over the courtroom, as everyone waits for the momentous entry. Nothing happens.

The lawyer then says, "The mere fact that you were watching that door, expecting the victim to walk into this courtroom, suggests that you have a reasonable doubt whether a murder was committed." Pleased with the impact of the stunt, he then sits down to await an acquittal.

The jury is instructed, files out and files back in ten minutes later with a verdict finding the defendant guilty. Following the proceedings, the astounded lawyer chases after the jury foreman to find out what went wrong. "How could you convict?" he asks. "You were all watching the door!"

The foreman explains, "Most of us were watching the door. But one of us was watching the defendant, and he wasn't watching the door."

"Did you know anything about this case?" the juror was asked.

"No."

"Have you heard anything about it?"

"No."

"Have you read anything about it?"

"No. I can't read."

"Have you formed any opinion about the case?"

"What case?"

"Accepted."

Juries

Juries scare me. I don't want to put my fate in the hands of twelve people who weren't even smart enough to get out of jury duty.

JUDGE: "What possible excuse could you have for acquitting the prisoner?"
FOREMAN: "Insanity, sir."
JUDGE: "What, all twelve of you?"

In Waterbury, Connecticut, Superior Court Judge Maxwell J. Heiman sentenced Richard C. Dobbins, Jr., to ten days in jail and fined him $100 for causing himself and sixty-six others in the jury pool to be disqualified from a triple-murder trial. When the court clerk called the roll of prospective jurors, each answered, "Here," except Dobbins, who yelled "Guilty!"

A man was on trial for murder, and the tide seemed to be running against him, so he tried to bribe an elderly juror to hold out for a verdict of manslaughter. The jury was out for three, four, five, six days, and the accused man's load of anxiety was nearly unbearable. But in the end, the jury brought in a verdict of manslaughter.

"Did you have much trouble getting the others to vote for manslaughter?" the man asked the old juror.

"You bet I did," the man replied. "They all wanted to vote for acquittal."

A jury is a collection of people gathered together to decide which side hired the better lawyer.

The jury was out for three hours in a very dramatic case. A husband had shot his wife's lover but only grazed his arm. The jury returned to the jury box and everyone in the courtroom awaited the verdict with bated breath.

The foreman of the jury, Mr. Tepperman, stood up. The judge asked the foreman whether they had reached a verdict.

"Yes," shrugged Mr. Tepperman, "we decided not to butt in!"

Every American believes in trial by jury—until he is called to serve on one.

Mrs. Hunter was called to serve for jury duty, but asked to be excused because she didn't believe in capital punishment and didn't want her personal thoughts to prevent the trial from running its proper course. But the public defender liked her thoughtfulness and quiet calm, and tried to convice her that she was appropriate to serve on the jury.

"Madam," he explained, "this is not a murder trial! It's a simple civil lawsuit. A wife is bringing this case against her husband because he gambled away the $12,000 he had promised to use to remodel the kitchen for her birthday."

"Well, okay," agreed Mrs. Hunter. "I'll serve. I guess I could be wrong about capital punishment after all."

COUNSEL: Can you tell us that you would follow the court's instructions regardless of what else happened to you during the course of the trial.

JUROR: Cognitively, yes. Rationally, yes. Emotionally, effectively, I don't know. Or perhaps effectively, yes, and rationally, no.

O'Sullivan, Cabot, Kelly, and Mendelbaum was one of the most successful law firms in New York. Of all the partners, Mendelbaum brought in the most business. Lunching with him one day, a curious friend asked, "Why is your name listed last. O'Sullivan spends most of his time in the south of France, Cabot is at his club's bar every afternoon, and Kelly is at the race track all the time. Since you bring in all the business, your name should be first."

Mendelbaum beamed. "All my clients read from right to left."

13

Law[s]

The law is the only profession which records its mistakes carefully, exactly as they occurred, and yet does not identify them as mistakes.

> Elliot Dunlap Smith,
> Conference on Teaching of Law in Liberal Arts
> Curriculum, November, 1954

Law—in its nature the noblest and most beneficial to mankind, in its abuse and debasement the most sordid and most pernicious.

> Lord Bolingbroke
> *On the Study and Use of History*: Letter 5
> (1739)

The bar is not a bed of roses—it's either all bed and no roses, or all roses and no bed.

> Rufus Isaacs

It has been frequently remarked with great propriety, that a voluminous code of laws is one of the inconveniences necessarily connected with the advantages of a free government.

Alexander Hamilton,
The Federalist No. 78 (1788)

Legislation in the United States is a digestive process by Congress with frequent regurgitations by the Supreme Court.

Sir Wilmot Lewis (attributed)

The practice of law in most courtrooms today is about as modern as performing surgery in a barbershop.

Gordon D. Schaber,
American educator; dean,
University of Pacific Law School,
San Francisco Examiner,
March 9, 1973

The table of contents of the ideal lawbook reads as follows:

Page 1–10	Libel laws
Page 11–24	Divorce laws
Page 25–36	Criminal laws
Page 37–359	Loopholes

People who love sausage and respect the law should never watch either one being made.

There are thirty-five million laws and no improvement on the Ten Commandments.

Law(s)

It would not be possible for Noah to do in our day what he was permitted to do in his own...the inspector would come and examine the ark and make all sorts of objections.

> Mark Twain
> "About All Kinds of Ships,"
> essay, 1892

It usually takes a hundred years to make a law, and then, after it has done its work, it usually takes a hundred years to get rid of it.

> Henry Ward Beecher, *Proverbs From Plymouth Pulpit* (1887)

In the United States, Congress makes the laws, the Supreme Court interprets them, the President executes them, and the citizens disobey them.

Alaska State Senator Bob Ziegler introduced a bill to make it illegal for a dog to impersonate a police dog. No dog other than a police dog could use police-dog facilities, eat police dog-food, bite criminals, or loiter in the vicinity of a hydrant.

Laws too gentle are seldom observed; too severe, seldom executed.

> Benjamin Franklin

14

Lawsuits

Hippodamus:

He maintained that there are three subjects of lawsuits—insult, injury and homicide.

Aristotle, *Politics*

Dear God:

My attorneys have advised me you are liable for the recent damage to the fence between Heaven and Hell."
Dear Devil:

Lacking legal counsel, I..."

Lawsuit: A machine you go into as a pig and come out of as a sausage.

Ambrose Bierce

Death is not the end; there remains the litigation.

Ambrose Bierce

Litigation is the basic legal right which guarantees every corporation its decade in court.

David Porter

In 1984 Walter Debow won a judgment for $3.4 million in damages against the city of East Saint Louis, Illinois, for a wrongful beating he suffered while in city jail, but he was unable to collect, as the city had gone bankrupt. In 1990, as compensation, Debow was given title to the city's main municipal building and its 220-acre industrial park.

15

Lawyers

An attorney said, "Moses was a great lawgiver. But the way he was satisfied to keep the Ten Commandments short and to the point shows he wasn't a regular lawyer."

This house where once a lawyer dwelt,
Is now a smith's. Alas!
How rapidly the iron age
Succeeds the age of brass!

Erskine

The pope and a lawyer happen to die at the same time and are standing together at the gates of heaven. St. Peter says to them, "Ah, gentlemen, we've been expecting you. Your rooms are ready." He turns to the lawyer and says, "Excuse me for a moment while I take the pope to his room. I will return presently and will then show you to your quarters."

"Gee," says the lawyer, "I wouldn't mind tagging along with you while you take the pope to his room. That is, of course, if you don't mind."

"We would be delighted," says St. Peter, looking at the pope. The pope smiles, and they all proceed through the pearly gates.

The arrive at the pope's room, and St. Peter opens the door. The room has a twin bed, a couple of chairs, a little table, a thirteen-inch color TV, and looks pretty much like a room in a Holiday Inn.

Taking his leave of the thankful pope, St. Peter then escorts the lawyer to his room. He opens the door and the lawyer is shocked to see a palatial suite complete with balcony, king-size bed, spiral staircase, color TV console with remote control, stereo, VCR, plush carpeting, Jacuzzi, and a sauna. He is totally flabbergasted and says to St. Peter, "This room is terrific! But tell me, why is it that the pope, the leader of the entire Roman Catholic Church, got only a standard room, and I got this wonderful penthouse?"

"To tell you the truth," says St. Peter, "we have had many popes check in up here, but you're the first lawyer to make it."

A teacher says to her third-grade class, "Children, I'm going to ask each of you what your father does for a living. Bobby," she says, "you'll be first."

Bobby stands up and says, "My father runs the bank."

"Thank you," says the teacher. "Sarah?"

Sarah stands up and tells the teacher, "My father is a chef."

"Thank you, Sarah," she says. "Joey?"

Joey stands up and announces, "My father plays piano in a whorehouse."

The teacher becomes very upset and changes the subject to arithmetic.

Later that day, after school, the teacher goes to Joey's house and knocks on the door. The father answers it and says, "Yes? Can I help you?"

"Your son Joey is in my third-grade class," says the teacher. "What is this I hear about you playing piano in a whorehouse for a living?"

"Oh," says the father, "You see, actually I'm an attorney, but you can't tell that to an eight-year-old kid."

FARMER: An' how's lawyer Jones doing, Doctor?
DOCTOR: Poor fellow, he's lying at death's door.
FARMER: That's grit for ye; at death's door and still lying.

A man and his brother opened a law office at Idaho Springs under the firm name of "Ed. Wolcott & Bro." Later the partnership was dissolved. One of the brothers packed his few assets, including the sign that had hung outside of his office, upon a burro and started for Georgetown, a mining town farther up in the hills. Upon his arrival he was greeted by a crowd of miners who critically surveyed him and his outfit. One of them, looking first at the sign that hung over the pack, then at Wolcott, and finally at the donkey, ventured: "Say, stranger, which of you is Ed?"

In 1990, Dr. James M. Dabbs, Jr., a psychologist with Georgia State University, revealed that high levels of testosterone—which causes overly aggressive or antisocial behavior—is commonly found in juvenile delinquents, substance abusers, rapists, bullies, dropouts, and *trial lawyers*.

More than half the presidents of the United States—a country burdened with huge debt, a devastating crime rate, a failing educational system, excessive acid rain, and an embarrassing series of World Cup performances—have been lawyers.

When the Shriners convened in Los Angeles one year, a main boulevard was roped off for their their climactic parade, and only official cars, prominently marked "Potentate," "Past Potentate," and the like, were permitted to use the thoroughfare for hours preceding the big march. One smart lawyer, anxious to avoid a detour that would make him thirty minutes late for his golf game, devised a sign for his car that got him right through the police barrier and enabled him to sail majestically up the empty boulevard. His sign proclaimed: "Past Participle!"

To celebrate their fiftieth wedding anniversary, a dignified lawyer took his wife to Europe. Neither had been abroad before, but a more wordly and sophisticated junior partner volunteered to make their Paris visit a breeze. "I know the manager of the finest hotel on the Champs Élysées," he assured them. "I'll write him that you're coming." He did, too. "This gentleman has done a lot for me," is what he dictated, "so I want to be sure that you give him the best of everything: corner suite, room service, tips on where to go, etc., etc., etc."

The manager himself greeted the lawyer in Paris, and though he seemed a bit surprised to meet the wife, shrugged his shoulders and conducted the couple to their suite. Everything was lovely—including three young ladies, very scantily clad, who sat demurely in a row in the sitting room. "Who are they?" gasped the lawyer, blushing violently. "Ah, monsieur," the manager assured him, "it is as your friend requested. Those are the three et ceteras."

O judge not a book by its cover
Or else you'll for sure come to grief,
For the lengthiest things you'll discover
Are contained in what's known as a Brief.

J.P.C. 116 Just. P. 640 (1952)

Sometimes a man who deserves to be looked down upon because he is a fool is despised only because he is a lawyer.

Montesquieu, Persian Letters, XLIV

"A simple barefoot Wall Street lawyer."
> Harold L. Ickes—referring to
> Wendell Willkie as Republican
> presidential nominee. Ickes says
> he borrowed the phrase from
> columnist Jay Franklin (John
> Franklin Carter)

The fact that a lawyer advised such foolish conduct, does not relieve it of its foolishness.
> J. Emery
> *Hanscom v. Marston* (1890)

To protect his clients from being persuaded by persons whom they do not know to enter into contracts which they do not understand to purchase goods which they do not want with money they have not got.
> *Lord Greene. Lord Evershed Practical and Academic*
> *Characteristics of English Law 40* (1956), says
> Lord Greene was fond of quoting this old
> definition of a lawyer's function.

Your lawyer in practice spends a considerable part of his life in doing distasteful things for disagreeable people who must be satisfied, against an impossible time limit and with hourly interruptions, from other disagreeable people who want to derail the train; and for his blood, sweat and tears he receives in the end a few unkind words to the effect that it might have been done better, and a protest at the size of the fee.
> William L. Prossner, 1 *Jl. Leg. Educ.* 260

Lawyers

A felon on trial is concerned about his chances. His lawyer tells him, "Be calm. I'm a terrific lawyer. I'll prove to the jury that you were in Hong Kong when the crime was committed. I'll put on two doctors who'll prove that you were temporarily insane. I'll pay off two of their witnesses. I have two school buddies on the jury, and my wife's uncle is the judge. Meanwhile, try to escape."

A lawyer's wife was unhappy with the state of their home. The furniture was old and dirty, the drapes worn, and the carpet half eaten away. She demanded a complete redoing.

The attorney said, "Look, sweetheart. I just got a new divorce case today. As soon as I break up their home, we'll start fixing up ours!"

A funeral was being held. A latecomer sidled in and sat down next to a man who happened to be an attorney. Hearing the minister start to talk about Jesus, the latecomer asked, "What stage are we in?"

The lawyer answered, "He just opened for the defense!"

Professor of Law Samuel Siegel helped would-be attorneys understand how to tackle difficult cases. "When you're presenting a case, if you have the facts on your side, hammer the facts," Siegel advised. "If you have the law on your side, then hammer the law."

"What if you don't have the facts or the law," a student asked. "Then what do you do?"

"Well, in that case," responded Siegel, "hammer on the table."

Clothes may not make the man—but a good suit has made many a lawyer.

Legalese: An obscure language, based on Latin (and hopefully destined for the same fate), which lawyers use to prevent laymen from understanding what they're being charged with and for.

Daniel R. White

JUDGE: What is the prisoner charged with?
LAWYER: He is a camera enthusiast.
JUDGE: But you can't put a person in jail because he is crazy about taking pictures.
LAWYER: He doesn't take pictures, Your Honor, just cameras.

In an act that amazed the audience, a dog sat onstage and played several tunes on a piano. As the audience applauded, a larger dog came onstage, forced the smaller dog from its stool, and led it into the wings.

Backstage, the trainer told the theater manager, "That's his mother. She wants him to give up music and go to law school."

San Francisco Chronicle:

They will tear down the statues of Lenin. They will put up statues of Melvin Belli.

Last year in a process free of interference from either government, the American Bar Association selected a handful of Soviet lawyers to come to the U.S. to explore the nooks and crannies of our legal maze.

We know what this means: Nuclear war becomes impossible. Neither side could afford the lawsuit.

It's like the old joke—if there is one lawyer in a town, he starves, but two lawyers will do all right because they'll keep each other occupied.

Did you hear that Saddam Hussein took 5,000 lawyers hostage: He threatened to let one go every day until we stopped the war.

The story is told that when Congress passed legislation on automobile emission control some years ago, the first thing automakers in Japan did was to hire 2,000 more engineers. In Detroit, they hired 2,000 more lawyers.

C. Thorne Corse, San Francisco:
"When I grew up, in-house lawyers were 'kept' lawyers," jokes the sixty-three-year-old Mr. Corse. "The feeling was: "Those who can't do, teach. Those who can't teach, go in-house."

Did you hear about the litigation paralegal who died and went to hell?
It took her three weeks to notice the difference.

* * *

"PIZZA CONNECTION" TRIALS

The defense lawyers joke with (Alexander) about their past narcotics clients' ridiculously incriminating "encoded" conversations:
"How many acres is it?"
"Fifteen. Very good property."
"Bring one over. Let me look."

Alexander's real contribution is her disturbing depiction of the spectacle of criminal defense in the context of a megatrial. She keeps a running tally of sleeping jurors. No one juror makes it through the (seventeen-month) trial without sleeping through testimony. As many as six jurors (not counting alternates) appear to be asleep at one time. When the defense moves to dismiss an "ever-sleeping" juror, Alexander says, Prosecutor Martin protests to U.S. District Judge Pierre Leval that he does not think "apparent inattentiveness is real inattentiveness" and that he has never noticed a juror "actually, totally asleep."

* * *

Complaint to lawyer: "Your dog bit me last night."
Lawyer to complainant:
1) My dog doesn't bite.
2) My dog was locked in the garage last night.
3) I don't have a dog.

Scientist and lawyer discussing marvels of technology. Lawyer is asked to identify an invention that he would classify as "miraculous."
Answer: the thermos bottle.
Why the thermos bottle?
When you put hot things in it, it keeps them hot and when you put cold things in it, it keeps them cold.
So what's the miracle?
How does it know?

Lawyers

Washington Monthly opines "anthopologists of the next generation will look back in amazement...the most ambitious and brightest were siphoned off the productive work force and trained to think like a lawyer."

A snake and a mole bumped into each other. The mole said: "I've been blind since birth and I don't even know what I am." The snake said, "I've been blind since birth, too, and I don't know what I am either. Maybe we should feel around on each other and we can figure out what we are."

So the snake wrapped around the mole and said, "Well, you're small and furry, but you have a hard nose and long, sharp claws." "Oh, my god," said the mole, "I'm a mole!" Then the mole began feeling the snake. "You are slimy and low and you have no balls," said the mole. "Oh, my God," said the snake, "I'm a lawyer!"

Criminal defense lawyer Ron Slick has a unique legacy. Eight of his clients have been sentenced to die in California's gas chamber.

This is a death row record no prosecutor can match.

As his clients' cases wind their way through appellate courts, Slick's record has made him the talk of the defense bar. Some lawyers joke that he has his "own wing" at San Quentin. "A lot of people refer to him as Dr. Death," said John Yzurdiaga, president of the L.A. Criminal Courts Bar Association.

Mike Nichols' *Regarding Henry* is a serious drama whose plot works nicely as a lawyer joke:

If you erased the mind of a cold, ruthless, unethical attorney, could you make him over as a warm, caring, honest human being?

Yeah, but he'd have to give up his job.

A "NEAR LAWYER JOKE":

Young person is approached by the devil, who shows him the two paths in life to follow (the straight and narrow and, well, you know...). Also shows him hell, to which, as we all know, the latter path leads.

Young person observes masses of people enjoying all manner of earthly pleasures, possessing all the goods that one might want, and in general enjoying themselves immensely. Chooses the devil's path and becomes the stereotypical lawyer.

Years pass, no-longer-young person dies, goes to hell and is greeted by the devil. Is assigned to a cell, from which he observes people being subjected to all manner of hideous tortures. Is told that his will start in the morning.

Puzzled, the lawyer, who followed the devil's path to the very best of his ability, asks: "But what happened to what I saw when you showed this place to me years ago when you signed me up?"

Devil responds: "Oh, you must have been here during our summer associate program."

Lawyers

A man was sent to hell for his sins. As he was being taken to his place of eternal torment, he saw a lawyer making passionate love to a beautiful woman. "What a rip-off," the man muttered. "I have to roast for eternity and that lawyer gets to spend it with a beautiful woman."

Jabbing the man with his pitchfork, his escorting demon snarled, "Who are you to question that woman's punishment?"

Life is filled with hard decisions. For example...you are driving home from work and as you cross the bridge, you see an IRS auditor and a lawyer engaged in a terrible traffic accident. Both cars are ablaze and you would only have time to rescue one of them.

What do you do...go home and watch *Cosby* or *The Simpsons*?

I shouldn't complain. I once had a lawyer who was so clumsy, one time he threw himself on the mercy of the court—and missed.

Lawyer Michael L. Cook: "I worked seven days a week through college and law school so that I could work seven days a week as a lawyer."

There is a fence between Heaven and Hell. One day it fell down on Heaven's side and God complained. He said to Satan, "If you don't fix it, I'll sue." Satan said, "Fine, but where are you going to get a lawyer?"

I'll tell you how smart my lawyer is. He never graduated from law school. He was so smart, he settled out of class.

* * *

Variations on a theme:

You walk into a room and find Saddam Hussein, an angry Bengal tiger, and a lawyer—and you only have two bullets in your weapon. What do you do?
Shoot the lawyer twice.

A Marine breaks into a bunker in Iraq, finds Hussein, Gaddafi, and a lawyer. Realizing he has but two shots left in his already drawn pistol...
He shoots the lawyer twice.

* * *

He's a wonderful lawyer. So tenacious. One of his clients was hanged but even then he didn't give up. He sued for whiplash.

He only handles personal injury case. To him, justice doesn't wear a blindfold—it wears a bandage.

16

Lawyers and Money

As of July 1990, the Manville Personal Injury Settlement Trust was depleted of funds because *lawyer fees consumed 40 percent of the trust*—and this after claim payments were made to only the first 22,386 asbestos workers and their families. As a result, 130,000 more claimants will have to wait twenty-five years until the trust refills.

Then there's the lawyer who in 1980 bragged that while en route from New York to San Francisco to take care of a matter for IBM, he used the airborne hours to work on a General Motors case—and billed *both* IBM *and* General Motors $250 an hour for the time he was airborne.

Two cleaning ladies who worked in a large law office building were talking one night.

"You know," one said to the other, "yesterday I asked an attorney on the third floor if I should wash his windows—and he billed me $65 for his time!"

A corporate executive received a monthly bill from the law firm that was handling a big case for his company. It included hourly billings for conferences, research, phone calls, and everything but lunch hours. Unhappy as he was, the executive knew that the company would have to pay for each of these services. Then he noticed one item buried in the middle of the list: "For crossing the street to talk to you, then discovering it wasn't you at all—$125."

Santa Claus, the Easter Bunny, a cheap lawyer, and an expensive lawyer were sitting around a table. On the table was a one hundred dollar bill. Suddenly the lights went out. When they came back on, the hundred dollar bill was gone. Who stole it?

Answer: The expensive lawyer.

Santa Claus, the Easter Bunny, and the cheap lawyer are figments of your imagination.

17

One Liners

Yuppie lawyers don't cry—they just Saab.

My lawyer had a bad accident. An ambulance backed over him.

Be frank and explicit with your lawyer....It is his business to confuse the issue afterwards.

J.R. Solly

Lawyers are like beavers: They get in the mainstream and dam it up.

John Naisbitt

He got his client a suspended sentence. They hung him.

Ever since three of his clients were hung, he's known as "Swing and Sway with Briefcase O'Shay."

He was admitted to the bar—then studied law.

She does settlement work. Her lawyer sues and she gets the settlement.

A lawyer is a man who advises his clients on how not to lose all they own to anyone but him.

Lawyers are a bunch of claim jumpers.

Love of justice in most men is no more than the fear of suffering injustice.

Francois, duc de La Rochefoucauld

There is no more independence in politics than there is in jail.

Will Rogers

Practice makes perfect, but with lawyers it is more likely to make them rich.

Ignorance of the law does not prevent the losing lawyer from collecting his bill

Anonymous

Did you hear about the lawyer who was so successful he had his own ambulance?

Lawyers sometimes tell the truth—they will do anything to win a case.

One-Liners

A judge is an attorney who stopped practicing law.

And is there anything more disgraceful than a judge who is disappointed...or, worse, dishonored?

Talk is cheap, but only if lawyers aren't doing the talking.

A lawyer's lawyer is one who names his daughter Sue.

Lawyer: One who protects us against robbers by taking away the temptation.

H.L. Mencken

Father works for a law firm. He makes loopholes.

Only a lawyer could write documents with more than ten thousand words and call them briefs!

Where else but the law can one person be a party?

One fine gent took a cab to bankruptcy court and named the cabbie as a creditor.

The differences between lawyer jokes and attorney jokes is about fifty dollars an hour.

Milton Berle

A lawyer helped a woman lose a hundred eighty pounds of fat. He got her a divorce.

Two very rich people got divorced, and their lawyers lived happily ever after.

His mother is Catholic. His father is Jewish. When he goes to confession, he brings along his lawyer.

Do unto others as you would want others to do unto you, or make sure you have a good lawyer first.

Playboy

How to tell when a lawyer is lying: His lips are moving.

Did you hear the one about the lawyer with a dilemma—he's got a great case, but there's no insurance on the other side.

Remember the old joke about the lawyer who proposed to his sweetheart, asking for her "hand in marriage—and all the appendages thereof?"

Headline:
Client was playing with new printer. Fake $20 bills just a joke, lawyer says.

By the year 2000, this country will have more lawyers than people.

Daniel White

A paternity suit is what happens when you leave the scene of an accident.

One-Liners

Lawyer—a cat that settles differences between mice.

In law, nothing is certain but the expense.

Samuel Butler

When the government puts teeth into a law, they are not always wisdom teeth.

Possession is nine points of the law, and lawyers' fees are the other ninety-one points.

Truth is stranger than fiction, especially in lawsuits.

Just think of the endless litigation that will arise when the meek inherit the earth.

18

Politicians

Winston Churchill was once asked to name the chief qualification a politician should have. His reply: "It's the ability to foretell what will happen tomorrow, next month, and next year—and to explain afterward why it didn't happen."

Fax machines can have a great effect on politicians. Somebody just sent a fax message to every member of our state legislature. Each fax message was exactly the same: "The press has found out everything." Both houses of legislature emptied out within thirty minutes.

The people can change Congress but only God can change the Supreme Court.

George W. Norris, 1861-1944

As we watched Judge Clarence Thomas's Supreme Court confirmation hearings, all of the commentators said the same thing: "One of these people in the room is lying." Do you believe that? You've got two lawyers and fourteen senators in the room and only *one* of them is lying?

Jay Leno

Will Rogers once said it is not the original investment in a Congressman that counts; it is the upkeep.

John Kennedy made this interesting observation about the public's "image" of politics:

Mothers may still want their sons to grow up to be President, but, according to a famous Gallup poll of some years ago, some 37 percent do not want them to become politicians in the process.

There's an old legend about the politician who looks out his window and sees his constitutuents marching by. "There go my people," he says. "I must hasten to find out where they're going so I can get in front and lead them."

From *The Reagan Wit*:

I've never been able to understand how the Democrats can run those $1,000 a plate dinners at such a profit, and run the government at such a loss.

Dallas, TX, October 26, 1967

Politicians

One way to make sure crime doesn't pay would be to let the government run it.

> Dallas, TX, October 26, 1967 Speech to the California State Bar Association:

Politics is supposed to be the second oldest profession. I have come to realize that it bears a very close resemblance to the first.

> At a business conference, Los Angeles, CA, March 2, 1977

*   *   *

POLITICIAN: "Now, ladies and gentlemen, I want to tax your memory."
VOICE IN AUDIENCE: "Good grief! Has it come to that?"

Politician: 1. a person who will stand for anything that they think will leave them sitting pretty. 2. a person who works their gums before an election and gums up the works afterward.

Politician: a person who is willing to do anything for the working class, except become one of them.

Jay Leno says, "I saw a senator on a Sunday morning talk show who said actions of the Senate have created jobs for a lot of citizens. Yeah, but let's face it—you can't make a career out of jury duty."

> Quoted in *The Wall Street Journal*

A politician sometimes knows the right thing, sometimes does the right thing, but most often just says the right thing.

Politics: the gentle art of getting votes from the poor and campaign funds from the rich, by promising to protect each from the other.

Oscar Ameringer

19

Presidents

JOHN ADAMS

I have lived long enough, and had experience enough of the conduct of governments and people, nations and courts, to be convinced that gratitude, friendship, unsuspecting confidence, and all the amiable passions in human nature, are the most dangerous guides in politics.

To Robert R. Livingston,
1/23/1783

CALVIN COOLIDGE

In a letter to his father dated January 28, 1901, Calvin Coolidge wrote:

"I was duly reelected to the office of City Solicitor. There were a couple of Irishmen after the job. They made me some trouble but they did not secure votes enough. I have business enough to get a fair living, but there is no money in the practice of the law. You are fortunate that you are not still having me to support. If I ever get a woman someone will have to support her, but I see no need of a wife so long as I have my health."

DWIGHT D. EISENHOWER

"There was a man in Louisiana condemned to be hanged and under the state law he was allowed five minutes to give whatever last words he might choose to speak on that occasion. Well, he thought a moment and he says, "Well, I haven't got anything to say—get on with it." A man in the audience rose and said, "If he doesn't want those five minutes, Mr. Sheriff, let me have them, because I am running for Congress.""

> Speech at Stratford, Virginia,
> May, 1958

When a group in his office had become quite chaotic in its discussion of legislation before Congress, President Eisenhower said he was reminded of a cross-eyed judge who went into this court one day and found that he had a cross-eyed jury.

"What's your name" he asked the first juror.

The second juror replied, "John Jones."

"I didn't speak to you," the judge remonstrated.

The third juror chimed in, "I didn't say anything."

ULYSSES S. GRANT

I know of no method to secure the repeal of bad or obnoxious laws so effective as their stringent execution.

> First Inaugural Address, 3/4/1869

Undistinguished and often shabby in appearance, Ulysses S. Grant did not recommend himself to strangers by his looks. He once entered an inn at Galena, Illinois, on a stormy winter's night. A number of lawyers, in town for a court session, were clustered around the fire. One looked up as Grant appeared and said, "Here's a stranger, gentlemen, and by the looks of him he's traveled through hell itself to get here."

"That's right," said Grant cheerfully.

"And how did you find things down there?"

"Just like here," replied Grant, "lawyers all closest to the fire."

RUTHERFORD B. HAYES
Politics and law are (or rather, should be)—merely results, merely the expression of what the people wish.

> Letter 11/25/1885, *Diary and Letters*,
> IV, 177

THOMAS JEFFERSON
Referring to Congress: That 150 lawyers should do business together is not to be expected.

> Autobiography,
> 1/6/1821; *Writings*, I, 87

The study of law is useful in a variety of points of view. It qualifies a man to be useful to himself, to his neighbors and to the public. It is the most certain stepping-stone to preferment in the political line.

> To Thomas M. Randolph,
> 5/30/1790, *Writings*, VIII, 31

If congressmen talk too much, how can it be otherwise in a body to which the people send one hundred and fifty lawyers, whose trade it is to question everything, yield nothing, and talk by the hour?

It is well known than on every question the lawyers are about equally divided...and were we to act but in cases where no contrary opinion of a lawyer can be had, we should never act.

LYNDON JOHNSON

At the swearing-in ceremony of U.S. Attorney General Katzenbach and Deputy Attorney General Clark, the President began the ceremony by remarking that in his part of the country there was a saying:

A town that can't support one lawyer can always support two.

Washington, DC,
February 13, 1965

Addressing a U.S. Steelworkers' meeting in Pittsburgh, President Johnson took delight in introducing a Republican senator and a Republican congressman, both of whom were known as Johnson critics:

"This situation reminds me of that judge down in Texas during the Depression when they called him up one night, a state senator did, and said, 'Judge, we just abolished your court.'

"The judge said, 'Why did you abolish my court?'

"And the state senator replied, 'Well, we have to con-

118

solidate the courts for economy reasons. Yours was the last one created.'

"And the judge said, 'You didn't do it without a hearing, did you? Who in the devil would testify that my court ought to be abolished?'

"The state senator said, 'The head of the bar association.'

"The judge said, 'Let me tell you about the head of the bar association. He is a shyster lawyer and his daddy ahead of him was.'

"Then the state senator said, 'The mayor of the city came down and testified.'

"And the judge said, 'Let me tell you about that mayor. He stole his way into office. He padded the ballot boxes. He counted them twice. Who else testified?'

"The state senator said, 'The banker.'

"And the judge said, 'He has been charging usury rates like his daddy and his granddaddy ahead of him.'

"The state senator said, 'Judge, I don't think we should talk anymore tonight. Your blood pressure is getting up. The legislature did adjourn. Somebody did offer an amendment to abolish your court. I was kidding. No one testified against you at all. But I have fought the amendment and killed it. I thought it would make you feel better.'

"The judge said, 'I know, but why did you make me say those things about three of the dearest friends I ever had?'

"The moral of the story is that Republicans frequently say some of the ugliest things about some of the dearest friends they ever had, particularly in an election year."

JOHN F. KENNEDY

When John F. Kennedy made his brother Robert Attorney General in 1961, a great cry of "nepotism" went up across the land. Kennedy retorted, "I can't see that it's wrong to give him a little legal experience before he goes out to practice law."

There was much discussion after the President appointed his brother Attorney General. Mr. Kennedy recognized the fact that in the beginning many people were against his decision. Shortly after his announcement he joked:

"Speaking of jobs for relatives, Master Robert Kennedy, who is four, came to see me today, but I told him we already had an Attorney General."

A lawyer once wrote to President Kennedy and suggested that his crime-fighting brother, Attorney General Robert Kennedy, would make a better President. Kennedy responded, "I have consulted Bobby about it and, to my dismay, the idea appeals to him."

At a Washington dinner party shortly after his inauguration, President Kennedy paid tribute to Washington lawyer Clark Clifford, who had served as Mr. Kennedy's representative to the Eisenhower Administration during the period of transition immediately after Mr. Kennedy's election.

"Clark is a wonderful fellow. In a day when so many are seeking a reward for what they contributed to the return of the Democrats to the White House, you don't hear Clark clamoring. He was invaluable to us and all he asked in return was that we advertise his law firm on the backs of one-dollar bills."

February 1961

ABRAHAM LINCOLN

A persistent party member once appeared before President Lincoln and demanded appointment to a judgeship as reward for some campaigning he'd done in Illinois. The President, aware of the man's lack of judicial attributes, told him it was impossible. "There simply are no vacancies at the present time." Mr. Lincoln said.

The man left. Early the next morning he was walking along the Potomac when he saw a drowned man pulled from the river and immediately recognized him as a federal judge. Without a moment of hesitation he presented himself to Mr. Lincoln while the President was eating breakfast, told him what he had seen, and demanded an immediate appointment to the vacancy.

Lincoln shook his head. "I'm sorry, sir, but you came too late," said the President. "I have already appointed the lawyer who saw him fall in."

In his legal practice, Abraham Lincoln was never greedy for fees and discouraged unnecessary litigation. A man came to him in a passion, asking him to bring suit for $2.50 against an impoverished debtor. Lincoln tried to dissuade him, but the man was determined upon revenge. When he saw that the creditor was not to be put off, Lincoln asked for and got $10 as his legal fee. He gave half of this to the defendant, who thereupon willingly confessed to the debt, and paid up the $2.50, thus settling the matter to the entire satisfaction of the irate plaintiff.

A New York firm wrote to Lincoln, then practicing law, requesting information about the financial circumstances of one of his neighbors. The reply was as follows: "I am well acquainted with Mr. _____, and know his circumstances. First of all, he has a wife and baby; together they ought to be worth $50,000 to any man. Secondly, he has an office in which there is a table worth $1.50, and three chairs, worth $1.00. Last of all, there is in one corner a large rat hole which will bear looking into. Respectfully yours, A. Lincoln."

Many successful politicians have found that a good sense of humor can be invaluable. I like to think that finding areas of mutual agreement is what politics is all about. To bring together opposing points of view, it helps to have a person who can keep everything in perspective—one who can add a light touch to even the most serious of occasions. We've had quite a few yarn spinners in our halls of Congress, and even a good number in the White House. Abraham Lincoln, one of my great heroes, was known for telling stories with a punch.

To counter a charge that he had made some errors in judgment, Lincoln once told a story about a lawyer and a minister who were arguing.

As they rode down the road together, the minister said, "Sir, do you ever make mistakes while in court?"

"Very rarely," the lawyer sniffed, "but on occasion, I must admit that I do."

"And what do you do when you make a mistake?" asked the minister.

"Why, if they are large mistakes, I mend them. If they are small, I let them go. Tell me, don't you ever make mistakes while preaching?"

"Of course," said the preacher. "And I dispose of them in the same way you do. Not long ago, I meant to tell the congregation that the devil was the father of liars, but I made a mistake and said the father of lawyers. The mistake was so small that I let it go."

In law it is good policy never to plead what you need not, but you oblige yourself to prove what you cannot.

> Abraham Lincoln, To U.F. Linder,
> 2/20/1848. *Complete Works*, II, 3

One of Lincoln's favorite stories was about his career as a young lawyer traveling on horseback from one country court to another. Once, when an opposing lawyer objected to a certain juror because he knew Lincoln, Judge Davis overruled the objection because it was a reflection on Lincoln's honor. When Lincoln examined several jurors to see if they knew the opposing lawyer, the judge reprimanded him, saying, "Now, Mr. Lincoln, you are wasting time. The mere fact that a juror knows your opponent does not disqualify him." "No, Your Honor," Lincoln replied, "but I am afraid some of the gentlemen may not know him, which would place me at a disadvantage."

Commenting on a fellow lawyer, who always talked in a very loud voice, Lincoln remarked:

"Back in the days when I performed my part as a keelboatman, I made the acquaintance of a trifling little steamboat which used to bustle and puff and wheeze about the Sangamon River. It had a five-foot boiler and seven-foot whistle, and every time it whistled, it stopped."

In a letter recommending a young man applying for admission to the bar, Lincoln wrote the following note to a Judge Logan, a member of the bar's examining committee:

My Dear Judge:

The bearer of this is a young man who thinks he can be a lawyer. Examine him if you want to. I have done so and am satisfied. He's a good deal smarter than he looks to be.

Yours,
Lincoln

Lincoln made these comments about George Forquer, a political opponent who had accepted an appointment to a $3,000 a year job which afforded him the opportunity to build a home with a lightening rod, which was very unusual in those days.

"I desire to live, and I desire place and distinction; but

I would rather die now than, like the gentleman (Forquer), live to see the day that I could change my politics for an office worth $3,000 a year and then feel equally compelled to erect a lightening rod to protect a guilty conscience from an offended God."

Story by Abe Lincoln (as told by Gregory Peck):

A ten-year-old farm boy, it seems, rushes to his father and says that he has just seen his big sister and the hired man in the hayloft, taking off their clothes. He isn't sure what they're up to, but he is afraid that they are going to spoil the hay by doing what should only be done in an outhouse. The father says, ruefully—this is a country lawyer's joke, used when the evidence can't be denied— "Son, you've got the facts right, but you've come to the wrong conclusion."

FRANKLIN PIERCE

On the subject of Congress: "In a body where there are more than one hundred talking lawyers, you can make no calculation upon the termination of any debate and frequently, the more trifling the subject, the more animated and protracted the discussion."

THEODORE ROOSEVELT

No nation ever yet retained its freedom for any length of time after losing its respect for the law, after losing the law-abiding spirit, the spirit that really makes orderly liberty.

Speech at Galena, IL, 4/27/1900,

A man who never graduated from school might steal from a freight car. But a man who attends college and graduates as a lawyer might steal the whole railroad.

> Attempting to persuade his son
> to become a lawyer

HARRY S TRUMAN

If you tell Congress everything about the world situation, they get hysterical. If you tell them nothing, they go fishing.

> 7/17/50

Referring to a bill he vetoed on the last possible day, although he had intended all along to veto it, Truman said he felt like the blacksmith on the jury out in Missouri when the judge asked him if he felt any prejudice against the defendant. "Oh, no, Judge. I think we should give him a fair trial, then I think we ought to take the s.o.b. out and string him up."

> 6/26/50

WOODROW WILSON

I used to be a lawyer, but now I am a reformed character.

20

Puns

The first attorney wore a civil suit.

A noted lawyer, F. Lee Bailey, took postgraduate courses and got a third degree.

In 1932 a briefcase for attorneys was made from banana skins—for lawyers who wanted to appeal their cases.

The judge couldn't be disturbed at dinner because His Honor was at steak!

The late Fred Allen, in his halcyon vaudeville days, used to come out on the stage carrying a coat hanger. He would explain, "I'm on my way to the courthouse to see if I can win a suit."

From *The Complete Pun Book*, by Art Moger:

In 1932 a briefcase for attorneys was made from banana skins, for lawyers who wanted to appeal their cases.

A lawyer once represented singer Al Martino. Al brought his two brothers with him to lunch with the lawyer. When the bill was presented, the lawyer was heard to say, "Would you call this a three-Martino lunch?"

21

Riddles

You know why they bury lawyers in graves dug twelve feet deep?
  'Cause they heard that deep down, lawyers are good people.

What's the difference between a pothole and a lawyer?
  You'd swerve to avoid the pothole.

Why did the cucumber want a lawyer?
  It was in a pickle.

What do you look for if you have a lawyer buried up to his neck in sand?
  More sand.

Q. Why does Washington have the most lawyers per capita and New Jersey the most waste dumps?

A. New Jersey got first choice.

Q. Why are scientists using lawyers instead of rats in medical experiments?

A. There are more lawyers to begin with, they multiply faster, and laboratory personnel become less attached to lawyers than to rats. Then, too, lawyers will do many things rats won't.

Why does New Mexico have so many vultures and Washington have so many lawyers?

New Mexico had first choice.

Did you hear the one about the difference between a vulture and a lawyer?

The vulture eventually lets go.

How many lawyers does it take to change a lightbulb?

Depends. How many can you afford?

What's a lawyer?

Someone who makes sure he gets what's coming to you.

What happens when a lawyer becomes a godfather?

He makes an offer you can't understand.

What's the difference between a lawyer and a vampire bat?

One's a bloodsucking parasite and the other is a mouselike creature with wings.

Riddles

What do you call a thousand lawyers at the bottom of the ocean?
   A good start.

How do you get a lawyer out of a tree?
   Cut the rope.

What's the difference between a lawyer and a catfish?
   One's a slimy, garbage-eating bottom-of-the-river nuisance...and the other's a fish.

Where do lawyers live?
   In legal pads.

What's the difference between a successful lawyer and a down-and-out hooker?
   There are some things a hooker just WILL NOT do for money.

What's the difference between a lawyer and an onion?
   When you chop an onion, you cry.

What do you call one empty seat on a bus full of lawyers that plunges off a cliff?
   A wasted opportunity.

What's the difference between a lawyer and a football?
   You only get three points when you kick the football between the uprights.

What's brown and looks good on a lawyer?
   A Doberman pinscher.

How to you tell the difference between a dead lawyer in the road and a dead snake in the road?

There are skid marks in front of the snake.

How do you know that God, who created the world out of chaos and darkness, was a lawyer?

Because he made chaos and darkness first.

22

Sayings/Proverbs

It's no accident that all the people one truly despises are called "in-laws."

Folk proverb

Better to be a mouse in the jaws of a cat than a man in the hands of a lawyer.

Spanish proverb

"Virtue down the middle," said the Devil as he sat down between two lawyers.

Danish proverb

Lawyers and painters can soon change white to black.

Danish proverb

Ignorance of the law does not prevent the losing lawyer from collecting his bill.

Anonymous

As well open an oyster without a knife, as a lawyer's mouth without a fee.

Proverb

Fond of lawsuits, little wealth; fond of doctors, little health.

Judges are lawyers who knew a governor.

Saying

He who is his own lawyer has a fool for a client.

Proverb

Law is common sense as modified by the legislature.

The three proverbial roads to success at the bar—influence, a book, or a miracle.

Saying

23

Wills

Hear about the lawyer who believed in reincarnation?
In his will he left everything to himself.

He owes so much money, his will is made out to the small claims court.

The lawyer was reading the old man's will before a gathering of his survivors. As everyone listened attentively, he read the final paragraph: "And, to my nephew Randolph, who always said I wouldn't remember him in my will—Hello, Randolph."

"Being of sound mind, I spent all my money before my greedy relatives could get their hands on it."

The rich old dying man called his lawyer to him for the purpose of disposing of his worldly goods. "How many children have you?" the lawyer asked.

"That, sir," said the old-timer, "will be decided by the courts when my will is contested."

If it wasn't for wills, lawyers would have to go to work at an essential employment.

Will Rogers

Where there's a will there's a delay.

The nonsense of one man cannot be a guide for that of another.

Buller, J., *Smith v. Coffin* (1795)

But thousands die, without or this or that,
Die and endow a college, or a cat.
Alexander Pope,
Epistle 3, to Lord Bathurst (1732)

24

Witnesses

Mama had to go to court to settle an estate.

"How old are you, Madam?" asked the judge.

"Forty-one."

"Now just a moment! I recall that you were here in this very court seven years ago and you gave me the same age."

"Your Honor," said Mama primly, "I am not the kind of person I should give every time a different answer."

Ms. Pelsky was not looking at the ground, although she knew it was there.

A lawyer was cross-examining a witness. He asked:

"And you say you called on Mrs. Jones, May second. Now will you tell the jury just what she said?"

"I object to the question," interrupted the lawyer of the other side.

There was nearly an hour's argument between counsel and finally the judge allowed the question.

"And as I was saying," the first lawyer began again, "on May second you called on Mrs. Jones. Now what did she say?"

"Nothing," replied the witness: "She was not at home."

PROSECUTOR: Now, you have described McKenna and Pacheco as throwing firecrackers at you?
VICTIM: Yes. They put it in my ear.
PROSECUTOR: Did that explode?
VICTIM: Pardon?

"Mr. Witness, you're not telling the same story now that you did right after the shooting happened, are you?"

"No, sir."

"Well, how do you explain the difference?"

"Well," replied the witness, "I was talkin' then; I'm swearin' now."

In another court case, an old farmer was giving testimony that was so far fetched that the judge thought it best to warn him that he was in serious danger of perjuring himself.

"Are you aware," the judge asked, "of what will happen to you if you are caught lying under oath?:

"When I die I'll go to hell," the old man replied.

"Yes, but what else?" the judge asked.

The old man was puzzled for a moment. "You mean there's more?"

Senator Everett Dirksen told the story of the fellow who witnessed an automobile accident and was called upon to testify at the trial.

Counsel said, "Did you see the accident?"

He said, "Yes, sir."

Counsel asked, "How far were you away when the accident happened?"

He said, "Twenty-two feet nine and three-quarter inches."

Counsel looked at the court and looked at the jury and said, "Well, Smartie, tell the court and jury, how do you know it was twenty-two feet nine and three-quarter inches?"

He said, "When it happened, I took out a tape measure and measured from where I stood to the point of impact, because I knew some lawyer was going to ask me that question."

Milton Stein was summoned to court as a witness in an important criminal trial. After he was sworn in, the prosecuting attorney asked, "Where were you on the night of August 15th?"

"I object!" yelled the defense lawyer, leaping to his feet.

"Now, just a minute!" Milton interrupted before the judge could rule on the objection. "I don't mind answering. Let him ask."

Again the prosecutor asked, "Where were you on the night of August 15th?"

Once more the lawyer shouted, "I object!"

"Why are you objecting?" Milton called from the witness stand. "By me, a good citizen is supposed to answer all questions."

At this point the judge attempted to clear the situation. He addressed himself to the defense lawyer. "In view of the fact that you yourself called this witness to the stand, and knowing that he is favorably disposed toward your client, to say nothing of his willingness to answer the question, I fail to see why he should not be permitted to do so."

The defense lawyer shrugged, and the prosecuting attorney framed his question again. "For the third time, sir, where were you on the night of August 15th?"

"Who knows?" said Milton.

Testimony of a witness in a car accident case:

"I pulled away from the side of the road, looked at my mother-in-law, and headed over the embankment."

LAWYER: "Now, sir, did you or did you not, on the date in question, or at any other time, previously or subsequently, say or even intimate to the defendant or anyone else, alone or with anyone, whether a friend or a mere acquaintance, or in fact, a stranger, that the statement imputed to you, whether just or unjust, and denied by the plaintiff, was a matter of no moment or otherwise? Answer me, yes or no."

WITNESS: "Yes or no what?"

No attempt to catalog courtroom folly would be complete without malapropisms, like this one from a witness describing how he was beaten:

"Then he repeated the blows the second time, right to left side of face, left to right side. You know—the defendant is one of those guys who is amphibious."

Then there are the floundering interrogations of witnesses:

COUNSEL: Was there some event, Valerie, that occurred which kind of finally made you determined that you had to separate from your husband?

WITNESS: Yes.

COUNSEL: Did he try to do something to you?

WITNESS: Yes.

COUNSEL: What did he do?

WITNESS: Well, uh, he tried to kill me.

COUNSEL: All right. And then you felt that that was the last straw, is that correct?

Another witness, when asked if "you, too, were shot in the fracas?" answered, "No, sir—I was shot midway between the fracas and the navel."

Asked to identify himself, a witness in a case began pompously, "I employ myself as a surgeon."

"But does anyone else employ you as a surgeon?"

Then there was the lawyer who questioned a coroner about an autopsy he had performed:

COUNSEL: Do you recall approximately the time that you examined the body of Mr. Edgington at the Rose Chapel?

WITNESS: It was in the evening. The autopsy started about 8:30 PM.

COUNSEL: And Mr. Edgington was dead at that time, is that correct?

141